NATIONAL GEOGRAPHIC
KIDS

EVERYTHING ANCIENT EGYPT

EVERYTHING
ANCIENT
EGYPT

BY CRISPIN BOYER
with James P. Allen, President of the International Association of Egyptologists

SCHOLASTIC INC.
New York Toronto
London Auckland
Sydney Mexico City
New Delhi Hong Kong

CONTENTS

Maintaining truth, justice, and order was the job of the goddess Ma'at, one of ancient Egypt's many deities.

A golden seat fit for a pharaoh, this priceless throne sat undisturbed for 3,000 years in King Tut's tomb until Egyptologists found it in 1922.

INTRODUCTION

TOWERING PYRAMIDS!
TITANIC TEMPLES! MUMMIES PRESERVED IN SECRET TOMBS! The people of ancient Egypt knew how to leave their mark on history. This kingdom of farmers and craftspeople ruled by godlike pharaohs thrived for 3,000 years along the banks of the Nile River in northeastern Africa, site of modern-day Egypt. Its monuments and stone-etched messages endured another two millennia despite tomb raiders and the scouring desert sands.

The study of ancient Egypt—called Egyptology—is as old as the pharaohs themselves, but much of what we know about Egyptian kings and culture is relatively recent information. Translations of tomb inscriptions reveal how ancient Egyptians faced death. Modern technologies such as CAT scans and DNA testing show how they lived their lives.

Who built the pyramids and why? Was the boy-king Tut really murdered? And why did the ancient Egyptians mummify cats and birds—even lions—as well as people? Dig into this book and become an Egyptologist. It's time to learn EVERYTHING about ancient Egypt!

EXPLORER'S CORNER

Hi! I'm Professor James Allen. I'm the president of the International Association of Egyptologists. When I'm not teaching about ancient Egypt at Brown University in Rhode Island, I'm studying hieroglyphs—ancient symbols chiseled and painted on the walls of tombs and temples. Look for me in these pages, where I'll teach you about treasure, pyramids, and war in ancient Egypt.

A kingdom rich in gold, ancient Egypt is renowned for its treasures. Craftspeople fashioned gilded sculptures, masks, jewelry, and furniture for their godlike pharaohs.

1

LAND
OF THE
PHARAOHS

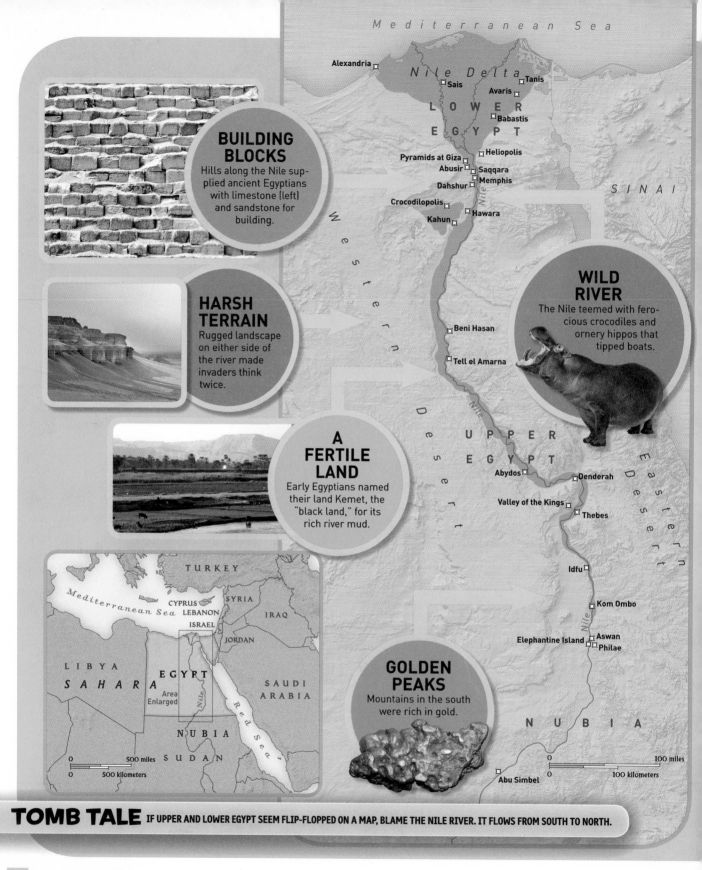

Mediterranean Sea

Alexandria

Nile Delta

Sais · Tanis

Avaris

LOWER EGYPT

Babastis

Heliopolis

Pyramids at Giza

Abusir · Saqqara

Dahshur · Memphis

Crocodilopolis

Kahun · Hawara

Western Desert

Nile

SINAI

Beni Hasan

Tell el Amarna

UPPER EGYPT

Abydos · Denderah

Valley of the Kings · Thebes

Eastern Desert

Idfu

Kom Ombo

Elephantine Island · Aswan

Philae

NUBIA

Abu Simbel

0 — 100 miles
0 — 100 kilometers

BUILDING BLOCKS
Hills along the Nile supplied ancient Egyptians with limestone (left) and sandstone for building.

HARSH TERRAIN
Rugged landscape on either side of the river made invaders think twice.

A FERTILE LAND
Early Egyptians named their land Kemet, the "black land," for its rich river mud.

WILD RIVER
The Nile teemed with ferocious crocodiles and ornery hippos that tipped boats.

GOLDEN PEAKS
Mountains in the south were rich in gold.

TURKEY

Mediterranean Sea

CYPRUS

SYRIA

LEBANON

IRAQ

ISRAEL

JORDAN

LIBYA

SAHARA

EGYPT

Area Enlarged

Nile

SAUDI ARABIA

Red Sea

NUBIA

SUDAN

0 — 500 miles
0 — 500 kilometers

TOMB TALE
IF UPPER AND LOWER EGYPT SEEM FLIP-FLOPPED ON A MAP, BLAME THE NILE RIVER. IT FLOWS FROM SOUTH TO NORTH.

THE GIFT OF THE NILE

IT'S HARD TO IMAGINE **A FLOOD CREATING ANYTHING** —except maybe a soggy mess. Five thousand years ago along the Nile River in northeastern Africa, however, floods fostered a great civilization. Swollen by rains in highlands far to the south, the Nile jumped its banks and soaked the surrounding fields every summer. When the water receded in October, it left rich black silt perfect for growing wheat to make bread and flax to spin linen for clothing.

This annual guarantee of good farming attracted herdspeople from the nearby desert. Soon, villages sprang up along the narrow strip of floodplain on both sides of the river. They organized into districts split between two distinct regions— Upper Egypt and Lower Egypt—known simply as the "Two Lands." Around 3100 B.C., the Two Lands united into the kingdom of Egypt, one of the world's first nations.

EXPLORER'S CORNER

The ancient Egyptians drew maps just like we do, but the one seen here is special—it's a treasure map! Part of a larger map now kept in an Italian museum, it shows the road from the Nile Valley through the eastern mountains to quarries and gold mines. There's no X marking the spot, but the map does have lots of notes in ancient Egyptian that highlight points of interest, such as "the mountains from which gold is taken." The map was found in the tomb of the man who drew it. He was a scribe named Amennakht, and he lived around 1150 B.C. in the village of workers who built the royal tombs in the Valley of the Kings.

Papyrus

RIVER GIVER

The Nile delivered more than just fertile flood mud to the Egyptians. Its other gifts included:

BRICKS: Riverbank mud was baked into bricks for houses and walls. Modern Egyptians still make them.

PAPYRUS: This miracle reed was used in everything from paper to boats to sandals.

SEASONS: Annual changes in the Nile divided the Egyptian calendar into three seasons: inundation, planting, and harvesting.

RELIGIOUS OUTLOOK: The Nile's annual renewal of the land influenced the Egyptians' views of life, death, and the afterlife.

TRANSPORTATION: Invented in Egypt, ships ferried people, goods, and building supplies throughout the kingdom.

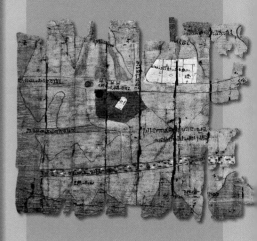

An illustration of an ancient Egyptian sun boat carrying a prince and his wife along the Nile

EGYPT UPS & DOWNS

"King Catfish" is seen uniting Upper and Lower Egypt on this slate from around 3100 B.C.

IT TOOK A STRONG LEADER TO UNITE

THE TWO LANDS OF EGYPT AROUND 3100 B.C. An ancient slate gives all the credit to a king named Catfish, although royal lists chiseled onto temple walls name a ruler later killed by a hippopotamus. Egyptologists aren't sure. Whoever he was, this mighty uniter established a kingdom that would last 3,000 years and become the region's dominant power.

But life in ancient Egypt wasn't always a bowl of figs (a favorite Egyptian fruit). Bad years were marked by discord between Upper and Lower Egypt, famine, plagues, or attacks by outsiders. Egyptologists call these not-so-great times "intermediate periods." They're sandwiched between stretches of prosperity known as "kingdoms." Egyptian history is further divided into dynasties for each sequence of rulers related by family (the famous King Tut, for instance, was a king in the 18th dynasty). Here's your key to the kingdom's major periods.

Early Dynastic Period
3100–2650 B.C.

A man from Upper Egypt named either Narmer ("Catfish") or Menes unites the Two Lands and begins the first dynasty of Egyptian kings. He rules from a new city called Memphis between Upper and Lower Egypt, but the capital will shift locations often throughout Egypt's history. Many aspects of the kingdom's long-lasting culture are established.

Old Kingdom
2650–2150 B.C.

Ancient Egypt makes great strides in mathematics, astronomy, art, and mummy making. But the Old Kingdom is best known as the age of pyramids, the most famous of which are guarded by the Great Sphinx at Giza. These mountain-size royal tombs are proof of the awesome power wielded by kings of this period.

Culture Crunching

2,000 years have passed since the fall of ancient Egypt.

4,000 years is how long China's culture has lasted, making it the world's oldest civilization.

3,000,000 people lived in ancient Egypt at the height of its power.

83,000,000 people now live in modern Egypt.

Middle Kingdom
2040–1640 B.C.

King Mentuhotep II reunites the kingdom. A fierce 12th-dynasty ruler named Senwosret III expands Egypt's borders into the gold-rich land of Nubia to the south. The afterlife becomes available to all Egyptians, not just kings. Art, jewelry, and literature reach new heights of quality. Later on, Egyptian children will learn to write by copying Middle Kingdom tales.

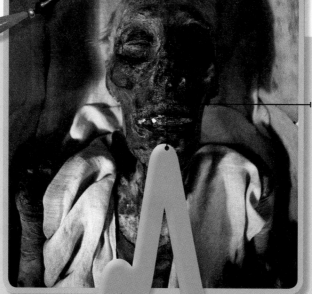

Egyptologists can learn a lot from a mummy. X-rays of Ramses the Great show that he suffered from arthritis and high blood pressure.

New Kingdom
1550–1086 B.C.

Warrior kings conquer new lands and bring the kingdom to the height of its power and influence. Many fascinating rulers—called "pharaohs" at this point in history— reign during the New Kingdom, including Ramses the Great, King Tut, and a queen who poses as a man. New monuments are built; old ones are restored. Pharaohs of this golden age are buried in the remote Valley of the Kings.

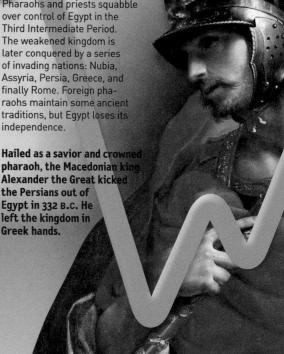

First Intermediate Period
2150–2040 B.C.

The Two Lands splinter as rival kings squabble. Political chaos gives the common people independence to create new art styles.

Second Intermediate Period
1640–1550 B.C.

Foreign settlers called the Hyksos take control of Lower Egypt and spark a war. They introduce the horse and chariot into combat and kill Egypt's King Seqenenre Taa in battle before eventually being driven out.

End of Ancient Egypt
1086–30 B.C.

Pharaohs and priests squabble over control of Egypt in the Third Intermediate Period. The weakened kingdom is later conquered by a series of invading nations: Nubia, Assyria, Persia, Greece, and finally Rome. Foreign pharaohs maintain some ancient traditions, but Egypt loses its independence.

Hailed as a savior and crowned pharaoh, the Macedonian king Alexander the Great kicked the Persians out of Egypt in 332 B.C. He left the kingdom in Greek hands.

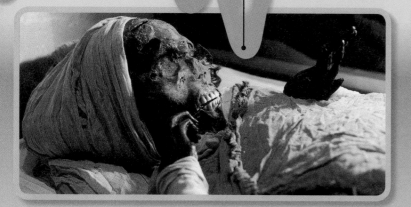

TOMB TALE A DAM COMPLETED IN THE 1970S FINALLY PUT AN END TO THE NILE'S ANNUAL FLOODING.

FOUR UNFORGETTABLE PHARAOHS

1 HATSHEPSUT
1479–1458 B.C.
Not happy co-ruling with her stepson, Thutmose III, this New Kingdom queen took matters into her own hands to become one of ancient Egypt's few female pharaohs. She commissioned artwork depicting the gods choosing her for the job, and she wore the male clothing and accessories—even the phony beard—of a king.

2 AKHENATEN
1349–1332 B.C.
Proof that pharaohs were all-powerful, King Akhenaten replaced the multitude of deities that Egyptians had worshipped for centuries with a single sun god named Aten. Together with his beautiful queen Nefertiti, Akhenaten built a capital city in the deity's honor while the rest of Egypt fell into decline. Akhenaten's famous heir, King Tutankhamun, restored the old gods. Akhenaten and Nefertiti's temples were soon demolished.

3 RAMSES II
1290–1224 B.C.
If you believe the inscriptions celebrating his life, Ramses II was a dashing warrior king who traveled with a pet lion and singlehandedly defeated an entire Hittite army during an ambush. Such tales tend toward exaggeration, but there's no denying that "Ramses the Great" was a revered pharaoh. This red-headed son of a commoner reigned for at least 65 years, built more monuments than any previous king, and outlived many of his 100 or so children.

4 CLEOPATRA VII
51–30 B.C.
This bewitching Greek queen became one of Egypt's most famous pharaohs—as well as its last. The first in her line of foreign rulers to learn the Egyptian language, she expanded the temples of knowledge in the Egyptian city of Alexandria. Her cunning and beauty won her the support of Rome—and the love of the Roman generals Julius Caesar and Mark Antony. Cleopatra and Antony famously committed suicide when Rome took control of Egypt.

THE GOD-KINGS

EGYPTIANS GOT WEAK IN THE KNEES WHEN THEY SAW THEIR KING, OR "PHARAOH," out and about. Lucky subjects were allowed to kiss his leg and foot. Everyone worshipped him like a god.

In fact, the Egyptians believed the pharaoh was a sort of living god. As the embodiment of Horus, the hawk-headed sky deity, the king had a private hotline to Egypt's group of fanciful gods. It was his job to establish temples and perform rituals to appease these deities and thus keep chaos from engulfing the Two Lands. Maintaining truth, justice, and order—a harmonious balance known as *ma'at*—ensured that the Nile flooded every year and the sun rose each morning.

On top of his religious duties, the pharaoh was in charge of Egypt's legal system and army. He married a queen and kept a harem of extra wives to help produce an heir. He lived in several opulent palaces with his royal family and employed an army of servants. Money wasn't invented yet, but the pharaoh was rich in things: grain, cattle, gold, giraffe skins, royal barges, and tributes from neighboring lands. He owned the kingdom and everything in it.

Revered kings were always portrayed on monuments as strapping young rulers no matter how they looked or how old they grew, but unpopular pharaohs received no such favors. Their names and likenesses were often erased from temples and columns by the kings who followed them.

Such rewriting of history makes it hard for Egyptologists to keep track of the roughly 170 kings who ruled ancient Egypt.

QUEEN NEFERTITI'S NAME MEANT "THE BEAUTIFUL ONE HAS COME."

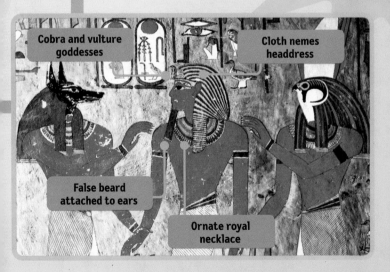

Cobra and vulture goddesses

Cloth nemes headdress

False beard attached to ears

Ornate royal necklace

Pharaoh fashion: Egyptian kings all wore the same royal raiment.

TOMB TALE THE TACTICS OF WARRIOR-KING THUTMOSE III ARE STILL STUDIED IN MILITARY ACADEMIES TODAY.

LAND OF THE GODS

ANCIENT EGYPTIANS

HAD A DEITY FOR EVERY DANGER, dilemma, and daily chore—more than 2,000 gods and goddesses. Some were local household gods who protected children and brought good luck. Others served as patrons of particular careers. Top gods were enshrined in massive temples that only priests could enter. The priests washed the gods' statues, brought them food, dressed them—even dabbed them with perfume.

All Egyptians tried to appease the gods by supporting truth, justice, and order (ma'at) in their lives. Maintaining ma'at kept the gods happy, and happy gods kept chaos at bay. The Egyptians believed all their gods and goddesses were simply different forms of a single creator that, according to one myth, spit them from the darkness long before Egypt was formed. Gods could look like animals or people—or a combination of both. Scan these two pages to see some of the kingdom's most amazing deities in their many forms.

Thoth
This god of writing, arithmetic, and wisdom took the form of a bird or a baboon.

Wadjyt
Many gods were tied to particular regions. The cobra-shaped goddess Wadjyt was associated with Lower Egypt.

Nekhbet
This vulture goddess was linked to Upper Egypt. Wadjyt and Nekhbet adorned the pharaoh's headdress to symbolize his rule over the Two Lands.

Re
This sun god came in numerous forms and was thought to travel across the sky in a boat. All the kings of ancient Egypt claimed to be his child.

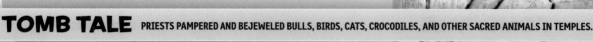

TOMB TALE PRIESTS PAMPERED AND BEJEWELED BULLS, BIRDS, CATS, CROCODILES, AND OTHER SACRED ANIMALS IN TEMPLES.

Devoted to Amun, the "king of the gods," the temple at Karnak in Thebes was the largest in all of Egypt. Pharaoh after pharaoh rebuilt and enlarged it over 2,000 years. It even had a zoo!

Bes
An itty-bitty household god with a big job, Bes protected Egyptian families from snakes and scorpions—even nightmares.

Sekhmet
Some gods were good. Some gods were bad. Some were both. The goddess Sekhmet was thought to spread disease— and cure it.

Horus
One of ancient Egypt's top gods, falcon-headed Horus was thought to walk the earth in the form of the pharaoh.

Ptah
Craftspeople worshipped Ptah, a mummified god thought to have created Egypt.

A PHOTOGRAPHIC DIAGRAM

THE TOMB OF SETI I

HERE'S A WALL-TO-WALL
GUIDE TO WHAT'S INSIDE the largest of the royal tombs carved into the limestone cliffs of the Valley of the Kings.

Stonecutter chiseling out chamber

Unfinished chamber

Stonecutter hauling out stones

Plasterer readying rough wall for artisans

Artist rendering a rough outline

Burial chamber

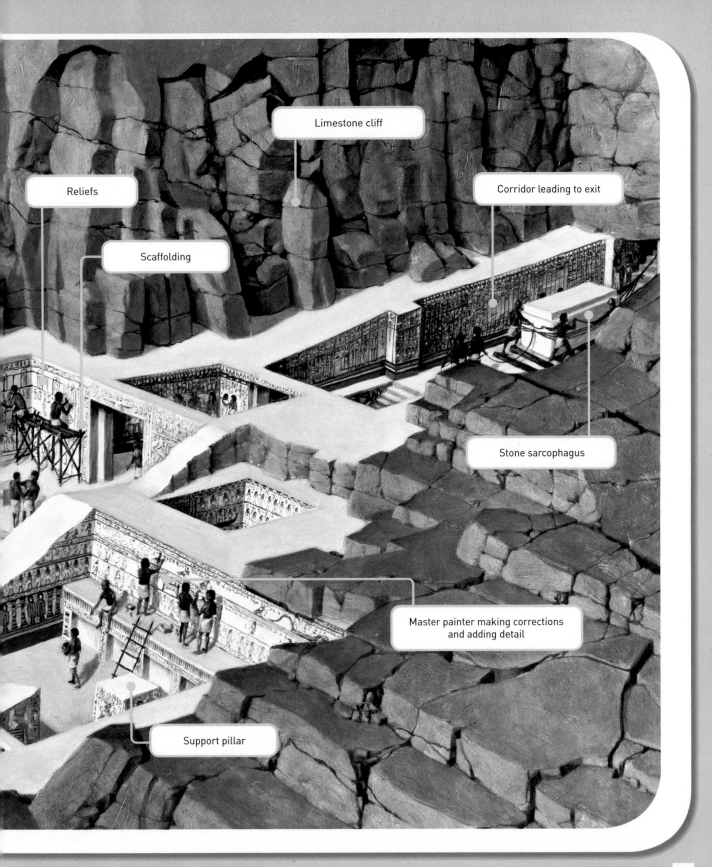

Limestone cliff

Reliefs

Scaffolding

Corridor leading to exit

Stone sarcophagus

Master painter making corrections and adding detail

Support pillar

2

DEATH
AND THE
AFTERLIFE

With the great forepaws of its lion's body stretched eastward, the pharaoh-headed Sphinx guards the second Great Pyramid of Giza. It was carved from rock over four millennia ago to honor the pharaoh buried in the pyramid.

MEET THE MUMMIES

It took 70 days to make a mummy. Some withstood the millennia better than others.

DEATH WAS JUST THE BEGINNING **FOR ANCIENT EGYPTIANS.** Fallen pharaohs were thought to become Osiris, the god of the dead. Ordinary Egyptians believed they would spend eternity visiting the living on Earth and shining among the stars with their ancestors.

But gaining entry into the afterlife wasn't easy. Ancient Egyptians believed that every person's spirit needed its body and a well-stocked tomb to survive in the hereafter, so they developed the process of mummification to preserve the dead. Mummies were placed in tombs that loved ones filled with food, clothes, and other offerings. If something happened to the mummy, its spirit could still dwell in a statue or a painting. For the craftsmen who made a living creating likenesses of the deceased, business was never dead.

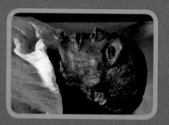

Embalming priests took pains to make mummies appear just as they had in life. Think you'll look as good as King Seti I here when your body is 3,300 years old?

HOW TO MAKE A MUMMY

Step 1: **NIP AND TUG**
Because mummy-making is a secretive—and smelly—business, priests carry the corpse to an embalming tent deep in the western desert. They wash the body and lay it on an embalming table. One priest

A priest of Anubis, the jackal-headed god of embalming, oversees mummification.

pushes an iron hook up the dead person's nose and pulls out the brain bit by goopy bit. Considered useless, the brain is thrown away. The body is sliced open, and its organs are removed.

BEST FRIENDS FOREVER

Archeologists combing Egypt have excavated an entire zoo's worth of preserved animals: cats, dogs, donkeys, lions, rams, hawks, shrews. Ancient Egyptians made these mummies for many reasons—not the least of which was companionship in the afterlife. Beloved pets were embalmed and entombed with their owners so they might reunite in the hereafter. One mummified man was buried with his faithful dog curled at his feet.

Sometimes, only an animal's meat was preserved to serve as an eternal jerky snack. Archeologists call these dried-up treats "victual mummies." Animals linked to specific gods were mummified by the millions. Crocodile mummies honored the fertility god Sobek. The mummies of long-legged Ibis birds represented Thoth.

An Egyptian farmer unearthed a mother lode of cat mummies in 1888. Considered worthless at the time, most were sold as fertilizer. Today, these everlasting animals are treasured and studied. They reveal the human side of ancient Egyptians, who loved their pets as much as we do. After all, would you want to face eternity without your furry best friend at your side?

An x-ray of this wooden cat coffin reveals a kitten entombed inside.

Not all animal mummies were legit. The baboon and cat here are preserved pets, but the tiny croc is a phony once foisted as a religious offering.

Step 2: DRY SPELL

The liver, stomach, intestines, and lungs are all carefully cleaned, preserved, and sealed in special "canopic jars" carved to look like the gods who guard these organs. The heart, however, is considered crucial equipment for the journey through the underworld, so it's put back into place. The body cavity is packed with an Egyptian salt called *natron* that soaks up all the moisture, and the corpse is left to dry for 40 days.

Step 3: WRAP ARTIST

The mummy-makers scoop out the salty natron and fill the body with spices, rags, and plants to maintain its human shape. The corpse is wrapped in layers of linen, giving it the famous bandaged look. Finally, the embalming priests tuck magical amulets into the wrappings and utter spells to activate their protective powers. The finished mummy and its canopic jars are delivered to the deceased's loved ones for a proper tomb burial.

TOMB TALE 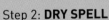 IT WAS A CRIME TO INJURE ANY EGYPTIAN—ALIVE OR DEAD—SO MUMMY-MAKERS CHASED AWAY THE PRIEST WHO CUT OPEN THE BODY.

PACKING FOR THE AFTERLIFE

BOATS

Egyptians believed the sun god traveled to the afterlife each night by boat. Entombed model boats—and even full-size versions—helped the dead make that same voyage.

IMAGINE HOW YOU'D FEEL IF YOU BOARDED A PLANE FOR A LONG TRIP

and realized you forgot to pack. To the ancient Egyptians, who viewed death as the start of a great journey, passing into the afterlife unprepared was equally unsettling. That's why family and friends filled the tombs of their dearly departed with everything they'd need in the hereafter.

Graves of poor Egyptians were packed with just the essentials: food, cosmetics, and clothes. The ornate burial chambers of pharaohs overflowed with treasures and art. Browse these grave goodies recovered from ancient Egyptian tombs.

FOOD

Family members left food offerings outside a tomb to nourish their loved one's spirit. Paintings of feasts on tomb walls or sculptures of food trays were thought to provide magical bottomless buffets.

CLOTHES

Most tombs were stocked with chests of clothes, fine linens, sandals, and other attire. It would be unseemly to spend eternity naked, after all.

CHARIOTS

King Tutankhamun's burial chamber contained six disassembled chariots so that the young pharaoh could charge through the afterlife.

TOMB TALE THE "BOOK OF THE DEAD" HAD SPELLS AGAINST EVERY AFTERLIFE UNPLEASANTRY, INCLUDING HAVING TO EAT ANIMAL POOP.

SURVIVING DEATH

Before finding eternal happiness in the hereafter, deceased Egyptians had to survive an underworld as treacherous as any video game, full of dangerous trials and demons with names like "Blood-eater" and "Demolisher." One wrong move would doom a poor soul to eternity in the netherworld.

Always planning ahead, Egyptians stocked their tombs with a strategy guide to beating this diabolical game. Called the "Book of the Dead" during the New Kingdom, it was a scroll packed with spells for defeating the demons. It even explained how to outwit the underworld's final boss, the jackal-headed Anubis, who examined each person's heart. Those who passed judgment could transform into spirits to visit the living. Hearts deemed unworthy were tossed to the Eater of the Dead, a demonic combo of a crocodile, lion, and hippo. In other words, game over.

COFFINS

Coffins were carved in the likeness of the deceased so that spirits could recognize their own bodies.

JEWELRY

The adage "you can't take it with you" would have horrified wealthy Egyptians, who packed their tombs with their favorite jewelry.

SERVANTS

Summoned to life by a spell, carved figures known as *shabtis* served as laborers in the afterlife. One pharaoh's tomb contained nearly a thousand of these ancient action figures.

GAMES

Board games like *Senet* provided eternal entertainment.

PYRAMID SCHEMES

AT THE DAWN OF

THE OLD KINGDOM, a brilliant Egyptian architect named Imhotep had a big idea. Unhappy with the boring brick structures that marked the tombs of previous Egyptian rulers, he designed a grave that gave his king a leg up to the afterlife. His "Step Pyramid" was a stack of six brick boxes that dwindled in size as they rose 200 feet into the sky. Created for King Djoser of the 3rd dynasty, it was the largest building in the world.

The Step Pyramid inspired subsequent rulers to build bigger and better tombs. A 4th-dynasty king named Khufu outdid everyone with his Great Pyramid at nearby Giza. Nearly half as tall as the Empire State Building when finished, Khufu's pyramid took more than 20 years to build with a workforce of 20,000. It held the title of world's tallest building for nearly 4,000 years.

More than a hundred pyramids were built after Khufu's, including neighboring tombs for his heirs and wives. By the Middle Kingdom, pyramid construction had become shoddy, and these expensive tombs soon fell out of fashion. Still, Imhotep's big idea had spawned ancient Egypt's most awe-inspiring monuments. By the Middle Kingdom era, Imhotep was worshipped as a god of wisdom and healing.

King Djoser's Step Pyramid (above left) inspired the straight-sided design of the Bent Pyramid (below left) 30 years later. Pyramid building achieved towering perfection with Khufu's Great Pyramid at Giza.

EXPLORER'S CORNER

The idea of pyramids originated at the very start of ancient Egyptian history. The earliest kings were buried beneath rectangular buildings called *mastabas*. Some of these buildings had a mound of earth inside, and these mounds inspired the giant stone pyramids later used for royal tombs. Like the mounds of dirt over seeds in a farmer's field, the pyramids represented a source of new life for the king's spirit. The king's body lay beneath the pyramid like a seed, waiting to give new life to his spirit at sunrise each day.

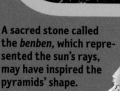

A sacred stone called the *benben*, which represented the sun's rays, may have inspired the pyramids' shape.

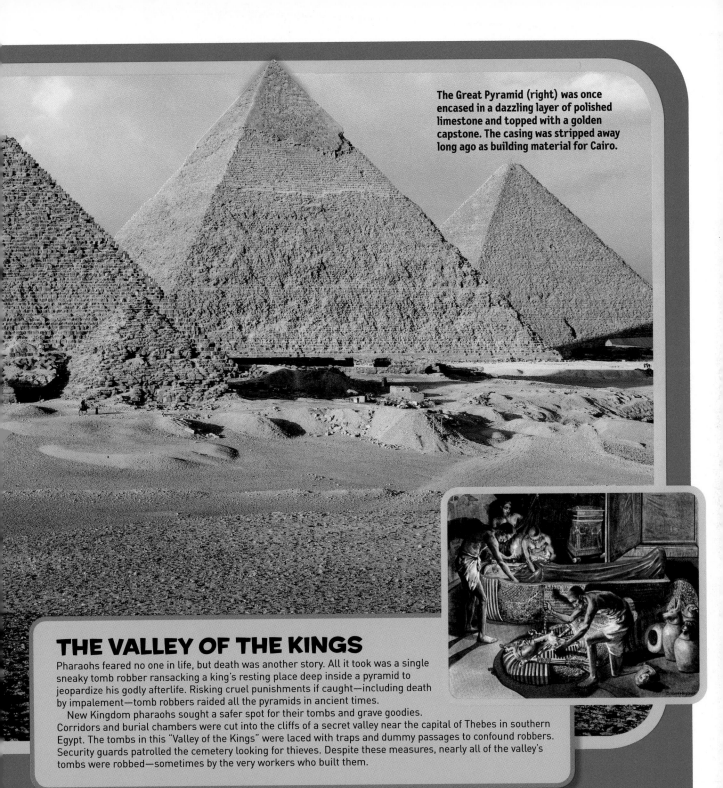

The Great Pyramid (right) was once encased in a dazzling layer of polished limestone and topped with a golden capstone. The casing was stripped away long ago as building material for Cairo.

THE VALLEY OF THE KINGS

Pharaohs feared no one in life, but death was another story. All it took was a single sneaky tomb robber ransacking a king's resting place deep inside a pyramid to jeopardize his godly afterlife. Risking cruel punishments if caught—including death by impalement—tomb robbers raided all the pyramids in ancient times.

New Kingdom pharaohs sought a safer spot for their tombs and grave goodies. Corridors and burial chambers were cut into the cliffs of a secret valley near the capital of Thebes in southern Egypt. The tombs in this "Valley of the Kings" were laced with traps and dummy passages to confound robbers. Security guards patrolled the cemetery looking for thieves. Despite these measures, nearly all of the valley's tombs were robbed—sometimes by the very workers who built them.

TOMB TALE OF THE SEVEN WONDERS OF THE ANCIENT WORLD, THE GREAT PYRAMID IS THE ONLY ONE LEFT STANDING.

THE TRUTH ABOUT TUT

Carnarvon (left) and Carter

CURSE OF THE MUMMY

Howard Carter's 1922 discovery of King Tut's tomb ignited a worldwide infatuation with everything ancient Egypt. When the sponsor of the Tut expedition, Lord Carnarvon, died less than a year after the tomb was opened, reporters pounced on the idea that he'd fallen victim to a mummy's curse.

In ancient Egypt, tomb walls were inscribed with curses to frighten away grave robbers. "To all who enter to make evil against this tomb," read one spell, "may the crocodile be against them on water and the snakes and scorpions be against them on land." But it wasn't crocs or scorpions that did in Lord Carnarvon—he died as the result of an infected mosquito bite. Carter, the man who broke the tomb's seals, lived for another 17 years.

To the ancient Egyptians, curses were real. Today, they make for a sensational story.

TREASURE! MURDER!

A MUMMY'S CURSE! Tantalizing tales swirl around Tutankhamun—aka King Tut—the most famous pharaoh of ancient Egypt. Archeologists have only recently begun to sort fact from fiction regarding the boy king's short life and mysterious death.

Like other New Kingdom pharaohs, Tut was entombed in the hidden Valley of the Kings. His rock-cut burial chamber is unique in that it hadn't been emptied by thieves. Instead, it sat largely undisturbed for millennia until Egyptologist Howard Carter discovered it in 1922. Archeologists a century ago weren't as gentle with mummies as they are today. They cut Tut into pieces to pry his body from his coffin. Such rough handling inflicted injuries on the

Using a digital version of King Tut's skull, artists created a flesh-and-blood model of the boy king. See any resemblance to Tut's golden funerary mask?

TOMB TALE BEFORE EGYPTOLOGISTS REALIZED THEIR VALUE, MUMMIES WERE USED AS TORCHES AND FERTILIZER—EVEN GROUND UP FOR MEDICINE!

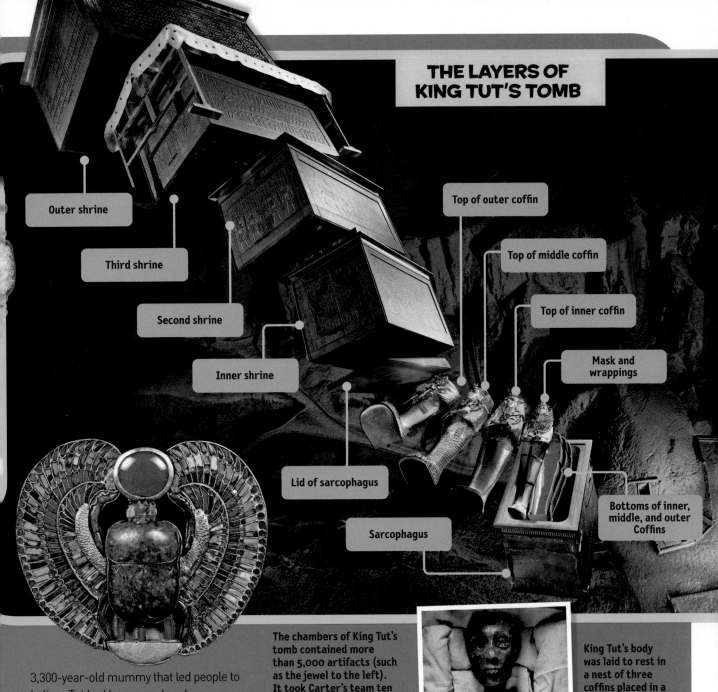

Outer shrine

Third shrine

Second shrine

Inner shrine

Top of outer coffin

Top of middle coffin

Top of inner coffin

Mask and wrappings

Lid of sarcophagus

Sarcophagus

Bottoms of inner, middle, and outer Coffins

The chambers of King Tut's tomb contained more than 5,000 artifacts (such as the jewel to the left). It took Carter's team ten years to catalog it all.

3,300-year-old mummy that led people to believe Tut had been murdered.

Modern technologies such as 3-D scanning and DNA testing paint a different picture. They reveal that the young king suffered from a bone disease and bouts of malaria that left him shaky and weak. None of the tests found foul play as the cause of Tut's death. The likely culprit is a broken leg that became infected. Perhaps the frail pharaoh—trying to appear as hearty as his ancestors—tumbled from one of the chariots found in his tomb.

King Tut's body was laid to rest in a nest of three coffins placed in a stone sarcophagus, which was covered by four overlapping, boxlike shrines.

A PHOTO GALLERY

GRAVE ROBBERS

BATTERED THE BODIES of entombed pharaohs to snatch their precious amulets, but true Egyptologists treasure mummies just as much as gilded grave goodies. Keep that in mind as you goggle at this gallery of the golden and the gross.

Shabti figures were inscribed with spells that set them to work in the afterlife. Some wielded tiny tools!

Even a pharaoh's toes, like King Tut's here, were preserved for the hereafter. If one broke off, a priest would replace it with a wooden toe!

A mummy's linen-wrapped face bears his likeness, ensuring that the spirit of the deceased will find his body.

Representing life, stability, and power, these three symbols were important for any pharaoh.

A mummified ram, one of ancient Egypt's many sacred beasts

The magnificent temple of Ramses II at Abu Simbel was relocated block by block to avoid flooding from the Aswan Dam.

Relief sculptures line the walls of this dim corridor in the Temple of Hathor. Egyptian artists would have used pottery lamps with linen wicks for light.

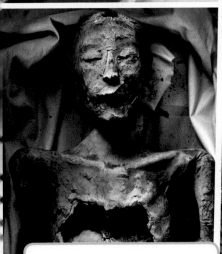

Faces of the love-goddess Hathor peer from atop towering columns in the well-preserved Dendera Temple complex.

Archeologists have discovered the mummy of King Tut's mommy, who was also his aunt!

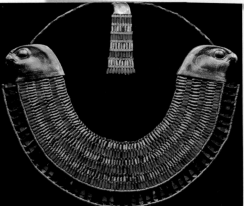

Funerary masks—such as this one for a noblewoman—reproduced a mummy's features in solid gold.

King Tut's name is encircled by a *cartouche,* a sacred symbol used to identify pharaohs, queens, and officials.

This gold-and-bead necklace was one of many "wonderful things" Egyptologist Howard Carter found in King Tut's tomb.

Farming in ancient Egypt was easier than in other parts of the world. The river delivered soft soil ready for planting.

3

LIFE
IN ANCIENT
EGYPT

A DAY IN DEIR EL-MEDINA

EVERYONE HAD THEIR PLACE

IN ANCIENT EGYPT. The royal family lived in lavish palaces scattered across the kingdom, while farmers and laborers clustered in villages laid out willy-nilly along the Nile. Skilled workers had it better than most, as archeologists learned when they discovered the ruins of Deir el-Medina near Thebes. This walled town housed the artisans who crafted the Valley of the Kings during the New Kingdom. They left behind relics that help us recreate the sensations of Egyptian daily life.

THE SOUNDS

Deir el-Medina's bustling main street is noisy and narrow. You can reach out your arms and touch the whitewashed houses on both sides! Two people nearby argue over the price of some fish. Money hasn't been invented yet, so buyers barter with sellers to figure out fair trades.

Meanwhile, soft singing wafts from a nearby rooftop. "I'll go down to the water with you," the singer croons, "and come out to you carrying a red fish." It's another love song. You hear plenty of those in this town of artists.

More than 70 families lived in and around Deir el-Medina. It would have bustled on weekends, when the craftspeople returned home from the Valley of the Kings.

THE SIGHTS

Heading indoors to dodge the desert heat, you find yourself in a typical Egyptian home: a few dimly lit rooms and a basement for valuables, scarcely furnished because wood is scarce. Your bed—a brick platform—doesn't look very comfy! Niches in the mud-brick walls hold statues of gods and shrines to ancestors. Seeing them makes you feel safe.

What are these pottery shards piled near the family goat? They're letters! Few Egyptians know how to read, but you're the privileged child of craftspeople, so you've been learning. A laundry list is scribbled on one shard. Another tells your favorite ghost story. Uh-oh—this last shard is from your teacher. "Bring your chapter and come!" it says.

THE TASTES

Like all Egyptian workers, Deir el-Medina's craftspeople are paid in food. Emmer-wheat, barley, fresh fish, fruit, and veggies arrive daily via donkey. Village wives brave the heat of their open-air kitchens to bake bread that tastes like sourdough, seasoned with honey and a dash of desert sand. That stuff gets everywhere!

EGYPTIAN JOBS, TOP TO BOTTOM

PHARAOH AND THE ROYAL FAMILY
. . . .

VIZIER
The pharaoh's top adviser
. . . .

PRIEST
Appeaser of the gods
. . . .

SCRIBE
Writer and recorder
. . . .

CRAFTSPERSON
Any skilled artisan
. . . .

FARMER/LABORER
Worker who feeds and builds the kingdom
. . . .

THE SMELLS

Donkeys drop plops in the street. Dogs with names like "Brave One" or "Lively" lift their legs outside doorways. Beloved pet cats treat the village like a litter box. Add the aroma of human waste piling up in primitive toilets (a box of sand placed under a seat) and take a whiff at high noon. Town life in ancient Egypt stinks! Villagers who can afford it burn incense to mask foul smells.

You and your fellow Deir el-Medina's residents are clean people who bathe often in the Nile but must rely on water hauled in daily. At least your clothes don't stink—laundry workers scrub the sweaty linens clean in the Nile.

TOMB TALE
BARLEY WAS FERMENTED AND BREWED INTO A GOOPY BEER THAT EVERYONE DRANK—EVEN KIDS!

MAGICAL MEDICINE

ACTIVE INGREDIENTS

REMEDY RECIPES INCLUDED . . .

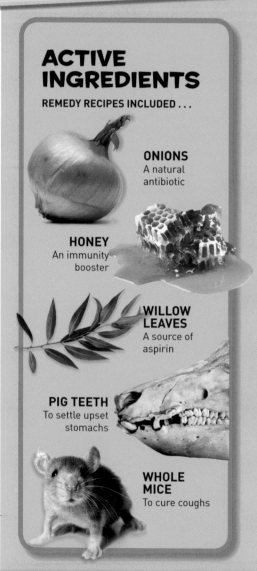

ONIONS
A natural antibiotic

HONEY
An immunity booster

WILLOW LEAVES
A source of aspirin

PIG TEETH
To settle upset stomachs

WHOLE MICE
To cure coughs

VENGEFUL GHOSTS AND NASTY DEMONS WERE THOUGHT TO CAUSE ILLNESS

in ancient Egypt, where magic and medicine went hand in hand. Doctors would utter spells to drive away spirits, then prescribe magical amulets—necklaces and trinkets—to protect sick people. They might even smear the patient's body with crocodile droppings to eject demons. After all, what self-respecting spirit would put up with that stinky smell?

Ancient Egyptian medicine wasn't all hocus-pocus. Doctors knew how to mix herbs into medicines that fought infection. They could mend broken bones and perform minor surgeries with scalpels made of razor-sharp rock or volcanic glass. Whatever the treatment or bizarre concoction, spells typically accompanied it. "Come you who expel evil things," went one incantation.

The men and women who treated the sick and injured were usually part-time scribes or priests who went to medical school at the temples. "The country is full of physicians," said the Greek historian Herodotus when he visited ancient Egypt. Rulers of foreign countries requested house calls from these healers for their unrivaled expertise. If you were to take ill in the ancient world, Egypt is where you'd want to seek treatment. Just tell the doc you prefer amulets to crocodile poop.

Lucky charms: Enchanted amulets offered magical protection.

TOMB TALE EGYPTIAN SAILORS BELIEVED THEY COULD WARD OFF CROCODILES JUST BY POINTING A THUMB AND INDEX FINGER.

COMMON AILMENTS AND CURES

EYE INFECTIONS: Blowing desert sand, swarms of flies, and Nile parasites left many Egyptians with irritated eyeballs.

The Cure: An ointment of honey mixed with human brains—and maybe a little dung—was applied to the eye. Fortunately, the eye makeup fancied by men and women also fought infection.

TOOTHACHE: Rocks used to grind grain left pebbles in bread, which wore down the teeth of ancient Egyptians.

The Cure: Sycamore fruit, beans, honey, minerals, and yellow pigment were mixed and applied to the sore tooth, likely resulting in a ghastly smile.

CROCODILE BITE: Although considered sacred, crocs were feared by Nile boatmen.

The Cure: Fresh meat was bandaged to the wound. Let's hope it was changed often!

BODY ODOR: Heavy labor in the desert heat naturally made for unfortunate fragrances.

The Cure: A mixture of incense, lettuce, fruit, and myrrh was rubbed on the smelly patient.

BROKEN BACK: Accidents were common on Egypt's colossal construction sites.

The Cure: A description of a crushed spine in a 3,500-year-old medical text offers this grim diagnosis: "not to be treated." Even Egypt's great doctors knew their limits.

DESERT DOC

History's first known physician is a man named Hesyra, personal doctor for the pyramid-building King Djoser. He wrote prescriptions and treated wounds just like a modern doctor.

ANCIENT EGYPT'S GREATEST HITS

Tomb paintings show musicians as popular craftspeople in ancient Egypt. At festivals and parties, they jammed together with flutes, lutes, harps, and trumpets, while dancers grooved to the beats of drums and a religious rattle called a *sistrum*. We don't know what their songs sounded like, but we do know the lyrics. Invent your own tune for this New Kingdom love song:

> *To hear your voice is pomegranate*
> *wine to me.*
> *I draw life from hearing it.*
> *Could I see you with every glance,*
> *It would be better for me*
> *Than to eat or to drink.*

TOMB TALE TO REMAIN PURE FOR THE GODS, PRIESTS PLUCKED ALL THEIR HAIR—EVEN THEIR EYELASHES!

ARTS AND CRAFTSPEOPLE

LIFE IN ANCIENT EGYPT

WASN'T ALL TOMBS AND GLOOM. The people of the Two Lands produced beautiful paintings, sculptures, furniture, and jewelry. But while ancient Egyptian art is world famous, most of the men and women who made it are not. They didn't sign their work like modern artists do. They didn't even call themselves artists—the word didn't exist!

Egypt's skilled painters, carpenters, and sculptors often worked for the pharaoh's government, decorating tombs and temples and producing royal grave goods. In their time off, they crafted trinkets for their homes or to trade for luxuries. Making masterpieces was a team effort. Sculptors handed their carvings to painters, who dabbed them with colored paste made from minerals. Draftsmen drew outlines on temple walls. Colorists painted within the lines. Sculptors chipped away the backgrounds to create a sense of dimension.

Artists followed strict rules to imbue their work with magic. If a painting adhered to sacred proportions, it would spring to life in the afterworld. Craftspeople were so convinced of their masterpieces' magical powers that they painted scorpions without their stingers!

Artists loved molding cups, amulets, and animals out of *faience*, a ceramic made from crushed quartz.

Kings were portrayed as perfect specimens (above) until the "heretic pharaoh" Akhenaten (left) ushered in a realistic art style.

Considered the sacred flesh of the sun god, gold was used mostly in royal jewelry. It was often inlaid with semiprecious stones such as turquoise and lapis lazuli.

Papyrus comic strips of predatory animals partying with prey show that ancient Egyptians loved a good laugh.

EGYPT AT WAR!

ANCIENT EGYPT BEGAN AS A KINGDOM **OF FARMERS, NOT FIGHTERS.** Peaceful trade with nearby nations ensured a supply of wood, incense, animal skins, and other luxuries. A full-time army wasn't needed during the Old and New Kingdoms, when village walls and Egypt's own natural barriers provided ample protection. Preferring diplomacy, pharaohs only went to war when push came to shove.

That shove came in the form of foreign invaders known as the Hyksos, who took control of Lower Egypt during the Second Intermediate Period. When a Hyksos ruler complained that Thebes's sacred hippos were disrupting his sleep, he was obviously trying to pick a fight—Thebes was hundreds of miles away! War erupted, and the Egyptian soldiers soon realized they were outmatched. The Hyksos wielded longer-range bows, deadlier swords, and—most lethal of all—horse-drawn war chariots. It took a century for Egypt's army to update its arsenal and drive out the Hyksos.

With the Two Lands reunited at the start of the New Kingdom, Egypt established a well-trained military composed of foot soldiers and elite charioteers. Warrior pharaohs Thutmose II and Ramses the Great personally led divisions named after gods to conquer new lands and establish Egypt as a true empire. A military career was difficult but rewarding for young Egyptian men. They earned spoils for their bravery and a plot of land when they retired.

SHARP OBJECTS

The Egyptian army's arsenal included daggers, spears, scimitars, and axes of copper, bronze, and—strongest of all—iron. Advanced New Kingdom bows could fire arrows the distance of two football fields.

This chest, called a hunting box, depicts King Tut as a strong and fearless leader going into battle against a group of Nubian soldiers.

NUBIAN DEFENDERS

Fearful that death and burial abroad would lead to a lousy afterlife, Egyptians often hired foreign mercenaries to fight their battles.

HOLY HELP

Pharaohs going into battle (such as King Tut, depicted on the chest below) would be well advised to bring along a symbol of everlasting life, like the *ankh* (right).

EXPLORER'S CORNER

Most of ancient Egypt's wars were defensive—fought to protect the country from foreign invasion. After conquering the Hyksos at the end of the 17th century, however, Egyptian kings went on the offensive, taking their armies into Syria, Lebanon, and even faraway Iraq. These military campaigns were designed to establish a zone of control around Egypt to prevent future invasions of the country. Under Ramses II, a famous battle was fought against the Hittites in Syria. This led to the first peace treaty in history, which was inscribed on the walls of the Karnak Temple in Luxor.

TOMB TALE EGYPTIAN SOLDIERS ONCE CAPTURED A WALLED TOWN BY HIDING IN SACKS THAT THE ENEMY MISTOOK FOR SUPPLIES.

ANCIENT EGYPT COMPARISONS

NILE STYLE VS. STYLE NOW

CLOTHING STYLES

NOWADAYS CHANGE WITH THE

seasons, and even the most minor fashion infractions will earn you snooty stares. Planning to wear white after Labor Day? How tacky!

But in ancient Egypt, where everyone from farmers to pharaohs strove to maintain balance and order, change was worse than tacky—it was dangerous! Clothing designs stayed the same from the Old Kingdom to the New, and people wore white for over 3,000 years.

That doesn't mean Egyptian style was boring. The people of the Two Lands developed jewelry, makeup, and hairstyles that would make today's lady pop stars go gaga. See for yourself as we compare modern and ancient fashions from head to toe.

Today's street clothing would make you sweat in the desert. Women in ancient Egypt wore lightweight linen tunics with attachable sleeves for cooler evenings, while men wore simple kilts. Children ran around naked. The ornate, pleated outfits portrayed in Egyptian art were reserved for those who could afford them.

HAIRSTYLES

We spend a fortune on hairstyling products. Ancient Egyptians had a simpler solution: They shaved their heads. Hair made them hot and attracted lice. Wealthy Egyptians wore wigs. Children sported "sidelocks" on one side of their heads.

BEARDS

Egyptians thought beards were unclean, so men went clean shaven. Believing the gods had immaculate facial hair, pharaohs wore phony beards. Even the female pharaoh Hatshepsut donned this sacred accessory.

COSMETICS

Ancient Egyptians were as obsessed with looking—and smelling—good as we are. Both men and women applied eye makeup. Wigs were scented with goopy perfumes. Lotions protected skin from the dry desert air.

JEWELRY

Just like men and women today, ancient Egyptians adorned themselves with rings, necklaces, anklets, earrings, and trinkets crafted of gold, silver, and semiprecious stones. Diamonds and emeralds, however, hadn't been discovered yet.

SHOES

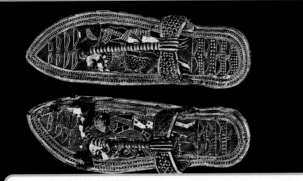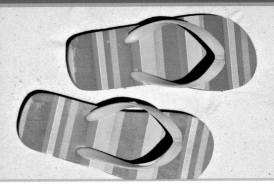

Egyptians didn't tie shoelaces. They trekked barefoot wherever they went and slipped on sandals only at the end of their journey. The soles of royal sandals depicted Egypt's enemies—the king symbolically trampled them with each step!

4

FUN
WITH ANCIENT
EGYPT

Sailing the Nile was the best way to get around ancient Egypt. A cruise across the kingdom could take as little as two weeks during the flood season.

Four feet long and weighing nearly a ton, the Rosetta Stone is inscribed with the same royal decree in three scripts: hieroglyphic, a shorthand version called *demotic*, and ancient Greek.

A scribe sat cross-legged and used his kilt as a writing desk. Exempt from taxation and heavy labor, he had one of the cushiest careers in the kingdom.

WRITE LIKE AN EGYPTIAN

LEARNING YOUR ABC'S

IS A BREEZE NOWADAYS, but what if the 26 letters of the alphabet were replaced with 700 pictures of animals and objects? Ancient Egyptians invented just such a script—later called hieroglyphic by the Greeks—around 3250 B.C. Inspired by the natural world, the famous symbols, called hieroglyphs, are etched across Egypt's ancient temples, tombs, and monuments.

Hieroglyphs at first portrayed precisely what they pictured. A symbol of a woman represented a woman. A pair of legs implied motion. Egyptian writers—called scribes—soon realized these hieroglyphs had limits. How do you draw jealousy? Or faith? So they developed symbols that represented sounds.

Hieroglyphs faded from use after the Romans took control of Egypt. By the 5th century A.D., nobody knew how to read them. The symbols remained a maddening mystery until 1799, when the French army discovered a granite slab near the Egyptian village of Rosetta. The stone was etched with a royal decree from 196 B.C., written in both hieroglyphic and Greek. By 1822, a French genius named Jean-François Champollion had cracked the code. Egypt's tombs, temples, and monuments could be read like a book!

MAKE YOUR OWN CARTOUCHE!

Give your hieroglyphic name the royal touch by drawing an oval around it like the one pictured. Called a *cartouche*, this sacred symbol was reserved for pharaohs, queens, and important officials.

CRACK THE HIEROGLYPHIC CODE! (See answer below.)

Hieroglyphic script is as complex as it is beautiful. Scribes in training spent years copying and recopying tales and prayers. When Egyptologists began decoding hieroglyphic they found that the script doesn't use vowels, so they had to fill in the blanks. Now it's your turn to do some detective work! Use the hieroglyph key to the left to decode the message on the ancient stone above. Keep in mind that hieroglyph sentences don't have punctuation or spaces, and they can be read in either direction. The animal symbols always face the start of the sentence.

TOMB TALE HIEROGLYPHIC HAD NO VOWELS, SO WE DON'T KNOW EXACTLY WHAT ANCIENT EGYPTIAN SOUNDED LIKE.

PLAY LIKE AN EGYPTIAN

AFTERLIFE OF LEISURE
Queen Nefertari, wife of Ramses the Great, plays an eternal game of Senet on the wall of her tomb.

IF YOU COULD PICK ANY PLACE IN THE ANCIENT WORLD TO

grow up, go with Egypt! Parents treasured their children—boys and girls—which wasn't always the case in other cultures. Sure, Egyptian mothers weighed their kids down with magical amulets, but children needed all the protection they could get against Egypt's many dangers, from lions on land to parasites in the water. And the toys! Egyptians spoiled their kids with balls, dolls, paintboxes, model boats, marbles, and wooden animals, not to mention exotic pets like hoopoe birds and baboons trained to pick fruit. Childhood was short, but kids still filled their free time with team sports, board games, and other fun activities.

Matters of Life and Death

5 years old was the age Egyptian boys and girls began working for their parents or started school.

14 years old was around when girls got married. Boys married when they were older.

40 years was the life expectancy of ancient Egyptians.

100 years was the possible age of Egypt's longest-reigning ruler, King Pepi II, when he died at the close of the Old Kingdom.

ACTION FIGURES

They may not have had Game Boys and Xboxes, but Egyptian children still had interactive toys with moving parts. Model animals were made with snapping jaws and wagging tales.

Play Tipcat!

To try this ancestor of baseball, you'll need a stick about 6 inches long with an oblong shape. It will serve as your cat, the "ball" in your game. If you can't track one down, ask your parents to taper the tips of a stick for you. Balance the cat on a flat stone or brick on the ground. Then take a baseball bat and lightly strike one of the cat's tapered ends to launch it into the air. (Wear sunglasses or safety goggles to protect your eyes.) While the cat's airborne, quickly whack it again to send it flying. Whoever knocks the cat farthest wins!

Play Egyptian Tug-of-War!

Always ready to roughhouse, children in ancient Egypt liked to grapple in wrestling matches, race on foot or in the water, and whack a leather ball with palm branches in a primitive game of hockey. So naturally you'd expect their version of tug of war to be more physical than what we play today. You won't need a rope to try it. Instead, members of each tugging team must form a human chain by clutching the waists or arms of their comrades. The leaders of both teams lock hands in an iron grip while their teammates haul backward with all their might. A team wins if it breaks the opposing leader's grip or pulls the other team across a line in the dirt.

Play Egyptian Board Games!

Egyptians loved playing elaborate board games with exotic names like Hounds and Jackals and *Mehen,* named for a serpent god. Their rules are long forgotten, but game experts have suggested modern equivalents you can try today. Hounds and Jackals, which has two players racing canine pieces around a tree, is similar to the kids' classic Chutes and Ladders. Senet, a pharaoh-favorite played on a rectangular board, is an ancient precursor to backgammon.

TOMB TALE CHILDREN WERE SO TREASURED IN ANCIENT EGYPT THAT PARENTS WHO COULDN'T CONCEIVE OFTEN ADOPTED.

DRAW LIKE AN EGYPTIAN

LOOK AT ENOUGH EGYPTIAN PAINTINGS AND YOU'LL NOTICE A FEW FUNNY THINGS.

The people they portray rarely look straight ahead. Pharaohs always tower over everybody else. And why are the poses so much alike?

From the Old Kingdom to the New, Egyptian painters adhered to an art style called "frontalism." Think of it as the opposite of today's 3-D movies—Egyptian artists believed a flat perspective portrayed people as clearly as possible. Paintings were a type of magic, after all, capable of animating in the afterlife. Eternity is no fun if you're missing a foot because of a bad artist!

For the magic to work, painters had to follow clear-cut guidelines—rules you can use to draw your own frontalism-style masterpiece. We've provided an example from the tomb of a well-to-do scribe as inspiration for your own creation. Just remember to follow these rules.

A GRID AND BEAR IT

The figures portrayed in ancient Egyptian paintings had to be properly proportioned or the gods wouldn't be pleased. To ensure these sacred design ratios, a draftsman first drew a grid over the work surface. You can replicate this first step by using graph paper for your drawing.

Each square in the grid is exactly the width of the main figure's hand. Your figure must stand 18 squares high from the soles of the feet to the hairline (seated figures are 14 squares tall). Knees are 6 squares high, and shoulders are 16. Feet are 3 squares wide. Shoulders are 6 squares wide.

B KEEP YOUR PERSPECTIVE

Always draw your figure's head in profile (looking to the side), with the eye fully drawn, as if it's peering at you. The chest and shoulders must be seen from head-on, while the hips are in mid-twist. Arms, hands, legs, and feet must be clearly shown (even the big toes of both feet should be visible). Choose a rigid pose. Figures in Egyptian paintings rarely look relaxed.

C SHOW RESPECT

Important characters are always drawn full size; everyone else is smaller. Only gods can rival pharaohs in size.

An illustration of a drawing board from the New Kingdom shows how Egyptian artists stuck to the grid.

SAVE FACE

Never draw anything obscuring a pharaoh's facial features. Ancient Egyptian artists came up with creative solutions for this rule, such as the behind-the-head arrow shot seen in the above scene.

CONSIDER YOUR COLORS

Use a reddish brown color for the skin of male figures and light yellow for skin of females. Choose your other colors carefully; they had meaning to the ancient Egyptians. Green represented new life, while red could stand for chaos. Black was the color of fertile soil and the underworld. Blue was used for the sea and sky.

GO WILD

Only human figures had to adhere to the rules outlined above. Feel free to draw animals in any wild style. The ancient Egyptians' fondness for the natural world is clear from the exquisite creatures portrayed in our sample painting.

TOMB TALE DON'T WASTE SPACE IN YOUR PICTURE WITH CAMELS—THEY WEREN'T INTRODUCED UNTIL LATE IN ANCIENT EGYPT'S HISTORY.

EGYPT
MYTHS VS. FACTS

WHICH OF THESE POPULAR IDEAS ABOUT ANCIENT EGYPT ARE FACT AND WHICH ARE MYTH?

A Slaves built the pyramids.

B Pharaohs married their own sisters.

C Royal servants were killed and buried with their king.

D Aliens helped Egyptians build their monuments.

E Napoleon knocked off the Great Sphinx's nose.

A **MYTH.** Pyramid builders were once portrayed as stooped slaves forced to haul heavy sledges by whip-wielding overseers, but slavery didn't appear in ancient Egypt until long after the Old Kingdom era. Instead, Egyptian farmers were drafted into a national labor force called the *corvée*, which handled the heavy lifting on pyramid construction sites during the flood season.

Such mandatory service might sound no better than slavery, but the government looked after corvée workers and their families. They were fed, clothed, housed, and given medical care when they got hurt. According to ancient graffiti, these men and women took pride in building a "house of eternal life" for their god-king.

B **FACT.** Pharaohs often took sisters, daughters, or other close relatives as their queens—a divine tradition inspired by their incestuous gods and to keep power within a single family. Osiris and Isis, two of ancient Egypt's most important deities, were brother and sister and husband and wife. Inbreeding took its toll on mere mortals, though. King Tut, whose parents were siblings, was frail and sickly.

C **FACT.** Archeologists have uncovered the bones of servants in burial pits near the tombs of Egypt's very first kings. These men and women were too spry to die of natural causes— they likely took poison at the time of their king's death so they could be with him. Fortunately for future generations of servants, flesh-and-blood laborers were eventually replaced with wooden shabti figures.

D **MYTH.** Some believe that ancient Egyptians couldn't possibly have cut, hauled, and lifted the massive limestone blocks used to build the pyramids with only the primitive tools and techniques available 5,000 years ago. Surely they had help! Some gods depicted in tomb paintings look suspiciously like alien visitors, after all.

Modern experiments using Old Kingdom construction methods, however, proved that pyramid building is possible without help from interstellar visitors. Scientists still debate what types of ramps were used and whether some blocks were cast from primitive cement, but they all agree that mere earthlings can build unbelievable things given enough time, manpower, and motivation.

The Luxor Hotel recreates ancient Egypt in the Las Vegas desert.

ANCIENT EGYPT EVERYWHERE

The aptly named Egyptian Bridge in St. Petersburg, Russia

A glass pyramid serves as the main entrance to Paris' Louvre Museum.

Hollywood's Egyptian Theater

You don't have to travel to Egypt to see pyramids and obelisks. The architecture and art styles of the kingdom on the Nile are all around us.

E **MYTH.** Someone gave the Great Sphinx the world's worst nose job hundreds of years ago, but it wasn't the French general Napoleon, who invaded Egypt in 1798 as part of France's war against England. The Sphinx actually lost its nose 400 years earlier, when a vandal pried it off in a fit of religious rage.

Tales of Napoleon's troops using the Sphinx's face for target practice are not only untrue but also unfair. Instead of destroying Egypt's ancient past, Napoleon's soldiers gave us the key to understanding it. Their unearthing of the Rosetta Stone marked the single greatest discovery in Egyptology.

Recognize the shape of the Washington Monument? It's an obelisk!

The Transamerica Pyramid, a San Francisco landmark

Flip over the U.S. dollar to find a familiar structure.

TOMB TALE FIRST DOMESTICATED IN ANCIENT EGYPT, CATS WERE ADORED—AND EVEN ADORNED WITH EARRINGS!

PHOTO FINISH

I WAS ASSIGNED TO

PHOTOGRAPH EGYPT'S OLD KINGDOM

for *National Geographic* magazine, and it quickly became clear that I would need a crash course in the more than 3,000 years of pharaonic Egypt. In a mere 80 years the three great pyramids at Giza, including all the queens' pyramids, were built by Khufu, Khafre, and Menkaure—and all of this was accomplished some 4,500 years ago with only copper tools.

I hired noted scholar and archaeologist Mark Lehner to guide me around and explain the overwhelming body of knowledge amassed by Egyptologists since the first European explorers of the early 19th century, including Napoleon Bonaparte on his conquering run through Egypt.

During one of my tours with Mark we were standing in front of the Sphinx, at the base of the causeway from Khafre's pyramid. Mark explained that while he was working on the restoration of the Sphinx in the preceding years, he happened to be there at sunset on the equinox. He observed that if you are standing directly on the axis, staring at the Sphinx, the sun sets directly on the corner of the Khafre Pyramid. For all the work that has been done at the Great Pyramids, no scholar in modern times had ever noted this amazing solar alignment—archaeoastronomy at its finest.

And the rest is history. I arranged to be there on the equinox in September and took this photograph. In the photography business "you have to make your own luck."

On the equinox, the sun sets on the corner of Khafre's pyramid when you are standing on the direct axis of the Sphinx.

AFTERWORD

ENDANGERED EGYPT

WORN OUT FROM HUNTING
LIONS IN THE DESERT, THE YOUNG PRINCE

scanned the sandy horizon for a shady spot to snooze. There, under the Great Sphinx! The prince knew his ancestors carved this amazing monument—part king, part lion—from a rocky outcrop over a thousand years ago. The intervening centuries had not been kind to the Sphinx. Its once-bold paint was faded. The shifting sands had buried its body to the neck.

The prince curled beneath the Sphinx's crumbling beard and fell asleep. Suddenly, the fatherly voice of the sun god spoke through the Sphinx, offering to make the prince into a pharaoh if he would just clear away the sand. "Do what must be done," the fading voice said as the prince awoke. His name was Thutmose IV, and he became Egypt's king around 1400 B.C. Archeologists know that Thutmose freed the Great Sphinx from the sand and patched its wind-blasted body.

Egypt no longer has pharaohs to look after its monuments. That duty falls to the country's Supreme Council of Antiquities, which must contend with threats King Thutmose never imagined.

Millions of tourists damage the ancient decorations. Air pollution from the great city of Cairo corrodes monuments. Water from farms seeps into foundations, causing hieroglyphs, carvings, and paintings to crumble. Ancient Egyptian history is being erased before our eyes.

Fortunately, the people in charge of preserving Egypt's past are working to limit tourism and human development's impact on the most endangered sites. And new irrigation systems are routing water away from temples and tombs. Whether these measures are enough to halt the damage to Egypt's monuments remains to be seen. If current conditions persist, the only way to protect the Sphinx might be to rebury it.

Imperiled by air pollution and traffic vibration from nearby Cairo, the Sphinx receives some tender loving care.

PROTECTING THE PAST

MODERN EGYPTIANS SEEM AS CONCERNED as anyone to preserve the past, both out of national pride and to protect the country's important tourism industry. During 2011's political revolt in Cairo, Egyptian citizens linked arms to form a ring around the Egyptian National Museum, protecting its priceless artifacts from looters. Such devotion gives hope that everything ancient Egypt will survive for another five millennia.

A modern Egyptian strolls through ancient Egypt in the temple at Karnak.

AN INTERACTIVE GLOSSARY

EGYPTOLOGY TERMINOLOGY

THESE WORDS ARE

COMMONLY USED among archeologists who study ancient Egypt. Use the glossary to learn what each word means and visit the pages listed to see the word used in context. Then test your knowledge of the Two Lands' lore!

Amulet
(PAGES 30-31, 36-37, 38-39)
A charm worn for its magical protective powers.

Along with amulets, what else would ancient Egyptian children wear for protection?
a. nothing. Clothing was optional for kids
b. thick boots resistant to scorpion stings
c. sheathed daggers given by their fathers
d. crowns decorated with cobra and vulture heads

Corvée
(PAGES 52-53)
The government's mandatory labor service, which provided manpower for building projects and the army.

Farmers were drafted into the corvée during the flood season because ___.
a. it was the coolest time of the year
b. their fields were underwater, so they couldn't farm
c. the flood season had the fewest religious holidays
d. all of the above

Dynasty
(PAGES 12-13)
A sequence of pharaohs related by family or marriage.

King Tutankhamun belonged to which dynasty?
a. the 10th
b. the 31st
c. the 18th
d. none of the above

Ancient Egyptian bigwigs as well as pharaohs were buried in ornate graves. Murals decorate this tomb of Sennefer, a mayor of Thebes.

Egyptologist
(PAGES 6-7)
A historian who studies ancient Egyptian culture.

The Egyptologist Howard Carter gained fame for discovering ___.
a. the Valley of the Kings
b. the Valley of the Queens
c. King Khufu's burial chamber in the Great Pyramid
d. the tomb of King Tutankhamun

Frontalism
(PAGES 50-51)
A long-lasting ancient Egyptian art style that portrayed people clearly in a 2-D perspective.

Which of these is a rule of frontalism?
a. always draw faces looking forward, with both eyes visible
b. animals must be portrayed from the side only
c. always draw a shield covering a pharaoh's head for protection in the afterlife
d. none of the above

Grave Goods
(PAGES 24-25, 30-31)
Supplies packed in a mummy's tomb to provide for the deceased's spirit in the afterlife.

Which of these items have been recovered from burial chambers?
a. entire boats
b. board games
c. mummified meat
d. all of the above

Hieroglyphic
(PAGES 46-47)
An ancient script composed of pictures that represent sounds, words, or concepts.

Scribes—the civil servants who could write in hieroglyphic—enjoyed which of these perks:
a. they didn't have to pay taxes
b. they never had to go to school
c. they didn't have to kiss the ground the pharaoh walked on
d. all of the above

Inundation
(PAGES 10-11)
The annual flooding of the Nile River and the name of the season when water covered the fields.

When the Nile River region was no longer inundated with water from heavy rains, the soil was perfect for growing ___.
a. rice
b. wheat
c. cotton
d. barley

Kingdom
(PAGES 12-13)
One of three prosperous periods in Egyptian history characterized by the unification of Upper and Lower Egypt under a strong king. The New Kingdom, for instance, was considered Egypt's golden age.

Intermediate Periods between the Kingdoms were marked by ___.
a. division between Upper and Lower Egypt
b. surpluses of grain
c. conquest abroad
d. all of the above

Ma'at
(PAGES 14-17)
A harmonious balance of truth, justice, and order. Also a goddess.

Why did Egyptians strive to maintain ma'at in their lives?
a. it kept the gods happy
b. ma'at held chaos at bay
c. it ensured that the Nile flooded every year
d. all of the above

Mummification
(PAGES 22-23)
The process of preserving an Egyptian's body for eternity.

Where could a deceased person's spirit reside after death?
a. in the dead person's mummy
b. in a statue of the dead person
c. in a painting of the deceased
d. all of the above

Papyrus
(PAGES 10-11)
A reed that could be sliced and pounded into a primitive sheet of paper.

What other materials did ancient Egyptians write on besides papyrus?
a. tomb walls
b. flakes of stone
c. shards of pottery
d. all of the above

Pharaoh
(PAGES 14-15)
The king (or queen) of ancient Egypt. The word originally meant "great house."

When did ancient Egyptians start referring to their king as pharaoh?
a. during the Middle Kingdom
b. during the New Kingdom
c. during the Second Intermediate Period
d. they always called him or her pharaoh

Sidelock
(PAGES 42-43)
A hairstyle common among Egyptian children, consisting of a long lock of hair sprouting from the side of an otherwise shaved scalp.

Facial hair in ancient Egypt was worn only by ___.
a. male pharaohs
b. female pharaohs
c. all of the above
d. none of the above

ANSWERS: Amulet: a; Corvée: b; Dynasty: c; Egyptologist: d; Frontalism: d; Grave Goods: d; Hieroglyphic: a; Inundation: b; Kingdom: a; Ma'at: d; Mummification: d; Papyrus: d; Pharaoh: b; Sidelock: c

FIND OUT MORE

Extend your stay in ancient Egypt with these websites, videos, games, and books.

WEBSITES

Tour Egypt
Dig deeper into the culture of ancient Egypt and plan a trip to its famous tombs and temples.
www.touregypt.net

National Geographic Explore the Pyramids
Learn how the pyramids were built—and meet the kings who made them.
www.nationalgeographic.com/pyramids

VIDEOS

Egypt's Lost Rival
National Geographic Channel Video, 2011

Engineering Egypt
National Geographic Channel Video, 2007

Egypt's Golden Empire
PBS Home Video, 2005

GAMES

Pyramid Builder
Design your own tomb—from its location to its building materials—when you visit www.bbc.co.uk/history/interactive/games/pyramid_challenge/index.shtml.

Senet
Play this ancient Egyptian board game at www.ancientegypt.co.uk/life/activity/main.html.

Mummy-Maker
Scoop out the brains and mummify the remains of a dead body at oi.uchicago.edu/OI/MUS/ED/mummy.html.

Tomb of the Unknown Mummy
Explore a creepy tomb with a lantern to discover who is buried deep inside. Play it at kids.nationalgeographic.com/kids/games/interactiveadventures/tomb-unknown-mummy.

BOOKS

Mummies
By Elizabeth Carney
National Geographic, 2009
Hold on to your lunch! The history of mummies comes to life through gruesome photos and fascinating facts.

Great Ancient Egypt Projects You Can Build Yourself
By Carmella Van Vleet
Nomad Press, 2006
Learn how to craft ancient Egyptian amulets, clothing, board games, and much more with this book of hands-on activities.

The Ancient Egyptian World
By Eric H. Cline and Jill Rubalcaba
Oxford University Press, 2005
An in-depth look at life in ancient Egypt, covering magic, medicine, famous pharaohs, Egyptian foods, and more.

Curse of the Pharaohs: My Adventures With Mummies
Zahi Hawass
National Geographic, 2004
Follow a famous Egyptologist as he explores ancient tombs and recounts his own experiences with mummy curses.

PLACES TO VISIT

Museum of Egyptian Antiquities, Cairo
Pyramids of Giza and the Great Sphinx, Giza
PlateauTemple of Karnak, Luxor
Abu Simbel, Southern Egypt